Much Love

To Your Self

From My Self ⤳

D.

1/26/2000

STRUTTERS & FRETTERS

WILLIAM STEIG

STRUTTERS & FRETTERS

OR

The Inescapable

Self

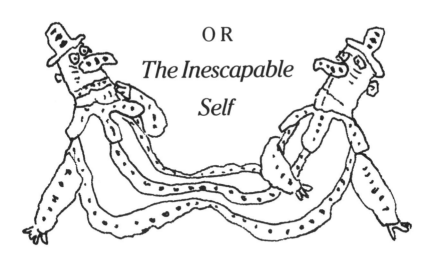

Michael di Capua Books • HarperCollins Publishers

FIRST EDITION

Designed by Janet Halverson

Library of Congress catalog card number: 92-70542

ISBN 0-06-118005-X

92   93   94   95   96   HR   10   9   8   7   6   5   4   3   2

When once the truth is grasped that
one's own personality is only a ridiculous
and aimless masquerade of something
hopelessly unknown, the attainment
of serenity is not very far off.

Joseph Conrad

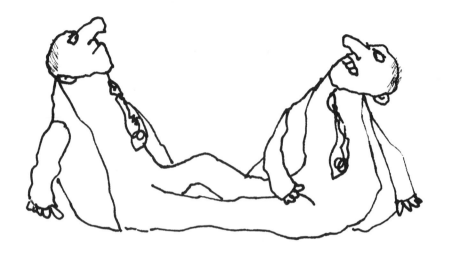

The Inescapable Self

He Knows His Rights

Clothes Make the Man

Intrepid Gambler

The Self as Something to Be Improved

Honoree

The Self Is Sensitive to Beauty

Possessions Are Part of the Self

Made for Each Other

The Self Is One's Chief Interest

Kindred Selves

A Self about to Enter a Room

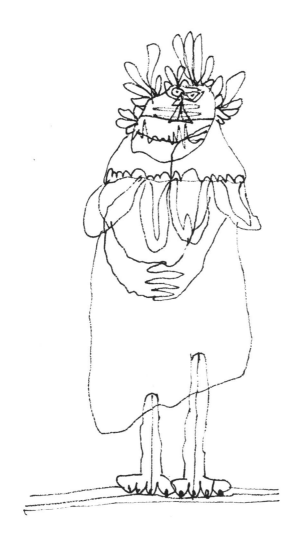

"What is your honest opinion of me?"

A Self on the Marriage Block

The Self Is Shy

The Self Has One True Friend

Initiate

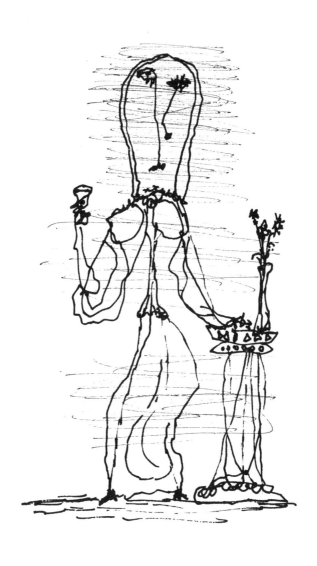

The Self Seeks Loss of Self

Incorrigible Villain

The Self at a Gathering

The Self Is a Role One Plays

A "Good Girl"

Self-conscious Self

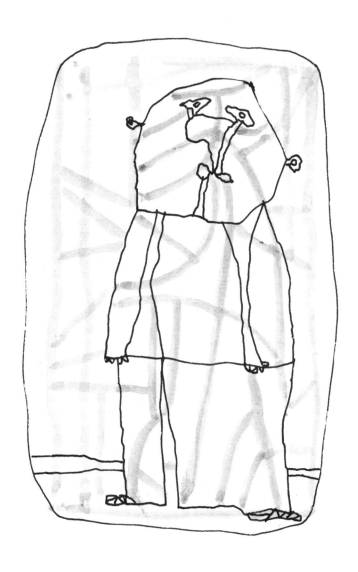

"I didn't ask to be born."

A Pair of Selves in Their Sunset Years

The Self Is a Big Baby

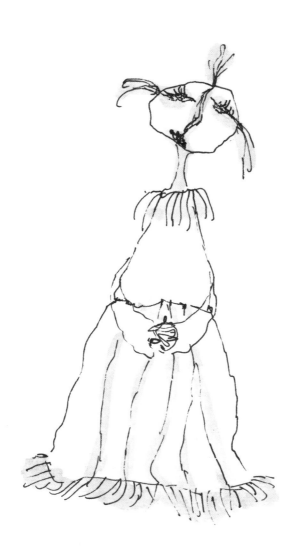

One Needs to Be Loved

Momentary Loss of Self

"What is your honest opinion of me?"

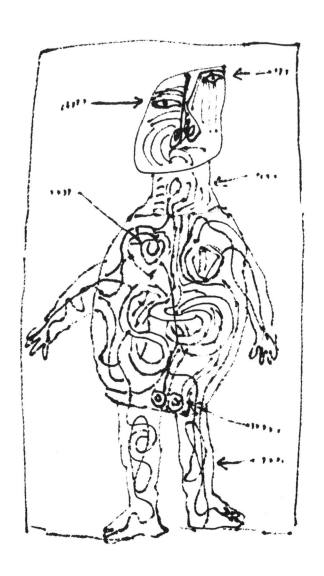

Hypochondriac

The Self Is Burdened with Sorrows

Lost Soul

The Self Feels Trapped in a Relationship

Recluse

The Self Has Found God

The Self Has Its Memories

Descendant of a Great Man

Femme Fatale

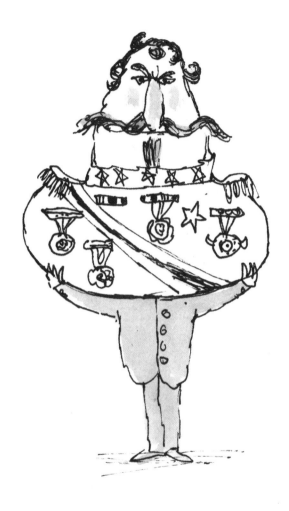

Egomaniac

The Self Is Obsessed with Sex

The Self Realizes What Might Have Been

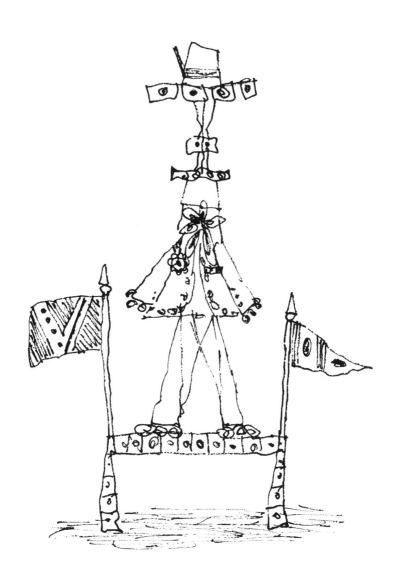

Loyalist

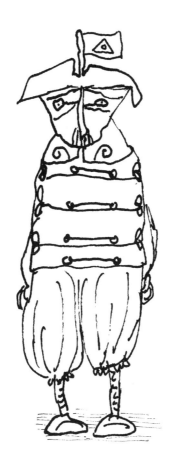

This Self Knows His Place

Self-discovery

The Self Can Be Dangerous

The Self Is Fiercely Competitive

The Self Has Criminal Impulses

A "Nobody"

One Whose Good Name Has Been Besmirched

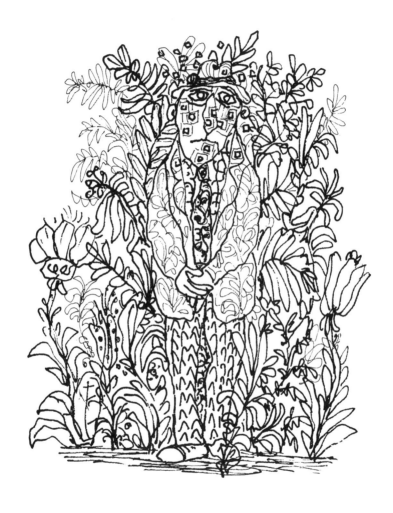

Self-effacing Self

Self-torment

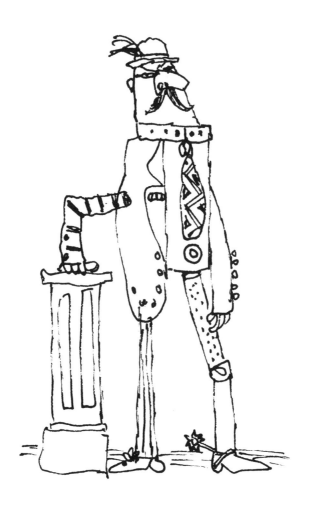

Man of Parts

Ego Trip

Spurned Lover

The Self Is Full of Fears

The Self Is Jealous

The Self Is Easily Offended

The Self Would Like to Belong

"What do you honestly think of me?"

Pawn

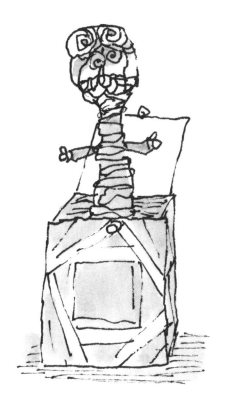

"Here I am!"

Veteran of Several Wars

Organism and Environment

One Has But a Moment on Life's Stage

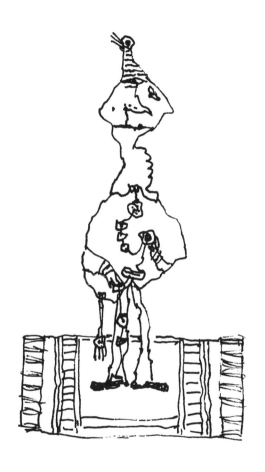

The Self Respects Authority

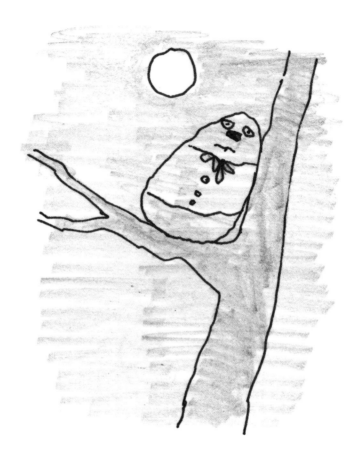

The Self Can Be Very Lonely

"Who am I?"

One's Mind Is Forever Chattering

Know Thyself

One Often Wonders What It's All About

The Self Is Reminded of Death

Somebody's Aunt

Member of a Secret Society

One Has Responsibilities to One's Self

A "Changed Man"

Man of Two Minds

Parting of the Ways

Great Self of the Past

The Self Finds Peace

Unwanted Child

"What is your honest opinion of me?"

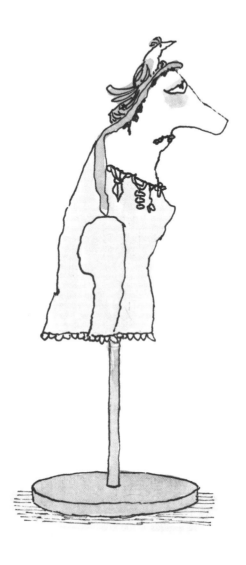

The Lovelorn Self

One Isn't Always as Good-looking as One Should Be

The Self Is a Butt of Humor

Father and Son

A Self in Love

Self-sufficient Self

The Self Is a Free Spirit

Deep Thinker

Somehow the Self Always Turns Up